In the Pockets of Small Gods

cx

Anis Mojgani

Write Bloody Publishing
America's Independent Press

Los Angeles, CA

Mojgani, Anis
1st edition.
ISBN: 978-1938912-84-9

Cover Design by Anis Mojgani
Interior Layout by Madison Mae Parker
Proofread by Florence Davies
Edited by Hanif Abdurraqib & Kaveh Akbar
Author Photo by Ryan Longnecker

Type set in Bergamo from www.theleagueofmoveabletype.com
Printed in California, USA

Write Bloody Publishing
Los Angeles, CA
Support Independent Presses
writebloody.com

To contact the author, send an email to writebloody@gmail.com
MADE IN THE USA

JMP

August 22, 1977- August 22, 2006

In the Pockets of Small Gods

I can see it like it was a film
                              with the January sun of Texas
smiling down on my skin and Burnet Road having
just finished eating tacos alone and just six blocks
from the house we had moved into together back
in October three years before—the little shitty one
that was dark but where the light in the bedroom
at the back would enter in so lovingly and where
I had set the kitchen on fire just before Christmas
, where we first brought Trudy home, and where
we would take her for walks together at dawn, at
dusk, and would often stroll down the street to the
same taco spot I was just now leaving when, after
six months of wishing I were dead, and only fifteen
miles from Lake Travis where Jeff chose to drown
now nine years past, from out of my dark steeping
heart the language changed, instead   *I want to kill
myself*   bubbled up to my damp brain for the first
time, as I crossed the street and sipped through my
straw cold black cherry soda and unlocked the car
door—windshield gleaming the same way I'm sure
the lake had when he left, with August dancing its
light across the top of the water like a blade traveling
slowly in the dream or a quiet ghost leaving its sheet—
and I lingered with the door open before the click
of the closing, on my arm the winter's sun so warm

//

I want to sleep the sleep of the apples
– Frederico Garcia Lorca

//

TABLE OF CONTENTS

•

Styx, Mississippi, whatever. Are we but names

///

When you're in your coffin, clanging down the river with all the other coffins in the water of the next world, all of them bumping and jostling against one another, the contents thrown about like riding in a small plane, you'll peek your head up to see what the racket is.

You'll see the other coffins. Looking around you'll see nothing but coffins and river and two banks distantly flanking the river, and the biggest tallest dark stretching above. So dark it feels like this place, big as it is, must be inside of some sort of bigger something. There are still stars though. Wherever this river is you can still see the stars.

While looking around you'll see that there are other heads peeking out of their coffins. You yell across the dark, asking:
you know where we are?

And someone will answer back: Nope, you?
Nope you say back.

You ask somebody else: What about you?
Nope. I wonder where this is.
And someone else will say: I don't know. It's big.
Yeah. Big.
Yeah. Big. It's vast.
And depending on what part of the river you're in, someone else may say:
Yeah. Vast like the backside of Sean Brown.

And even though no one knows who Sean Brown is, everyone will laugh. The chuckles will subside until a quiet sets in over the laughter, a quiet like you sat in somebody else's church. Like it's strange and it ain't for you or you don't get it but maybe you can see that somebody does and that it's for them or for some people—people who like you are just trying to house some sense of the world. So you lean into that understanding with respect. If not for the outcome at least for that desire to make a place special for finding the understanding.
And that's where the quiet comes from.

Someone will then ask someone else: Where you from?
And they will say: Texas. What about you?
Boston!
Boston?
Yeah, Boston.
I know someone from Boston. Kate Leigh. You know her?
No.
What about Stephen Ellis?
Nah. I'm actually in Somerville.
Somerville?
Yeah Somerville.
And someone else will then yell out: Somerville?
I know someone in Somerville!
Who?
Nick Kathkart! Know him?
Yeah! I do actually! I do know him!
Yeah?
Yeah!
Oh man, small world.
Yeah, Nicky's a great guy!
He is, he is. I hadn't seen him in five, ten years, and when I did he had a first edition of an e.e. cummings book to give to me. Great guy.

And the first person won't know who e.e. cummings is but will still agree that Nicky is a great guy. And then it will get quiet again. Until someone else asks: Where are we again?
And no one will answer.

A few people shrug. All of you will look into the stars that are collecting in the distance of the above. You'll try to think of someone you might know that lives in Somerville or Texas or Florida or France, just to have something to talk about with a person you never met before just right now, just to share something in the dark quiet, even though all of you are already sharing the river and the sound of the current bumping all of you into one another and you'll wonder where the water is taking you and how long it will be before it brings you there and what there will be like, if it'll be like here on the river with all of us sitting in our boxes trying to split the dark by sharing our voice with others, if it'll be like how it was in the world before this one.

///

I do not remember if it was August like his coming and his going but it must have been as July was when he was found

I remember spending all morning wondering if I needed to wear dress shoes or if I could wear my cream colored converse

I remember I sat near the back in a pew by myself

I do not remember if there was a coffin. If there was, there would have been nothing inside of it. I remember a picture of his face in a frame sitting on top of something

I remember his precious mother, never seeing her cry, how happy and grateful she was to have me there. I remember dandelions in the grass when we stood outside afterwards, when she and his father were shaking everyone's hands, how beautiful the two of them looked smiling inside the sun

I remember it was a beautiful day
—one of those perfect southern ones New Orleans can get

I remember thinking I had bet on the wrong horse

remember wanting to break his face open

I remember all this unnamed and nameless *this* that was in me
All this curdling blood and anger and want

And if I could tell my then self something now I would tell him
that the wolves in the woods sometimes make halos to better hold us and
sometimes the wolf makes the halos that we might be better held

I would say Anis—it is very possible for a person to be loved and yet still feel
so alone that they just have to leave

O Jeff

       what rattled inside the flower your chest held
                                  so tightly
that you had to go live once again back with the animals
                         o closeness that was you

You wore sandals
and emerald velvet to our prom
and so at the back of the church I sat with my dirty chucks on
their soles fresh with the morning soil and dew

I remember it was summer
I think I was wearing long dark sleeves
When I left the house to go
I couldn't feel any of the sunlight that the day dared
to try and touch me with

///

And when summer was leaving
I would lie in the garden and pretend I was a carrot

Would sometimes curl under the big leaves and become a head of lettuce

Sometimes in the softest earth I would bury my softer paws
and I was a rabbit

Sometimes when in the garden I was a rock
wishing I were two rocks
was sometimes becoming three rocks
was sometimes warmed by the sun or held
cool and smooth in a palm
and brought home to be placed
in the window light beside a person's bed

When in the garden as a rock
sometimes I waited hundreds of years
and it was only the wind that touched me

Sometimes I waited hundreds of years—thousands
of years!

and not even the wind could move me

Sometimes I would watch from the garden
to the birds gathering
to spell their bodies upon the clouds
while heading for weather
warmer than from where I watched

Sometimes when fall came someone would carve dates into my stone face
and I would stay keeping time with those that slept beneath me
gone into the grass of another world
And there were times when there I stayed
under the rock of the earth
all autumn long

just in case
those who were lost and dead needed me
to maybe find a way back home. And when winter came
the only way I knew I could still feel
was how cold the snow made me

So I stayed there. In the garden
And waited for spring
As the snow fell. To keep feeling
—cold as it was—
                    something
as it lay upon me

///

When she went she didn't just go, she went and with the harvest. And with the seeds for the next season, though with no intent to sow. Instead absentmindedly let them spill from the train window. And before heading to the station, salted the earth, all while trying to convince the gossips in the square that the blue and yellow house in the forest beside the bright field outside of town had actually been a dark house of falling wood, had actually never been. What house? A house, there? Painted the color of the sun? And the sea you say? No. You must have been dreaming. Mistook for maroon birds in the cobalt morning, the last bit of sleep echoing out of the dreaming. She always kept a pitcher of cold water beside the bed, to pour over her brow when she woke, to make sure nothing of what she had loved in her sleep lingered long enough to remember when stepping out of bed.

///

She told me she didn't want to be married anymore
while we ate pizza at the pizza place on Chavez
I had been waiting all summer to take her to.
It wasn't really a surprise. The past year
had been some strange universe
devoted to making me small enough to dissolve. But still
it hurt. Afterwards we went home and cried a lot
and laughed some and ate chocolate ice cream on the couch and then she
went somewhere else.
There is more to this story but not here.

•

I went to two movies today.
At the second one I ate a watermelon salad
while watching dirty men move through a moving train.
My teeth felt so soft and the inside of me
was passing through a long tunnel.
I started writing this poem while still in the tunnel.
It is light outside but I am in the tunnel.
There is a ballet happening without dancers, only music
and everyone watching an empty spotlight. Everything is a house
that birds fly into to die.

•

Inside the forest inside of me is a house with a man inside of it.
There are other houses throughout the forest,
which once housed neighbors
neighboring the home of the man. But they have all moved away
and the man is surrounded by all these empty houses.
One day a woman moves into one. She just shows up.
She sends a bird from her window to his, carrying a river stone in its feet.
He sends the bird back with a polished acorn.
They send gifts back and forth
until one day she comes over to introduce herself.
They talk and laugh. She goes back to the house she stays in.
A day or two later she comes back and again
a day or two after that. Soon they are together
every day. Soon they sing together and cook together
and walk through the woods together. Soon she stops
going home to her house. They sleep in the same bed.
He paints pictures of her where she has red hair
because he has red paint and she sits still with a smile
like she is watching a secret form before her. She undresses
and he moves the wet brush across her back. She sits quietly
reading on his couch holding her ankle in her right hand
and then holding her right hand around his left.
Soon it is her couch too. She has trouble falling asleep,
she kicks her legs restlessly. He has trouble staying asleep,
waking up gasping for air. There arms find each other. The owls circle
silently. And then one day she is gone.

•

And then once more it is just the man
in the middle of this forest of abandoned houses. He sits
with a stack of firewood and matches, wondering
which houses are worth burning to the ground. Wondering
if any of them are. And if so, if his house too should burn.

///

Every corner of my heart loved you

In a field of fields you were the largest field
In a field of moons you were the most moons

Sisyphus

///

The story goes like this: having eaten the girl's grandmother, the wolf then dresses up in the grandmother's clothes and disguised as the small girl's loved one, eats her. Wrapped in a cloak the same color as the inside of the wolf, the little girl's body becomes lost inside the beast, becomes only a voice trying to speak through stomach and skin. A woodcutter comes upon the wolf asleep in the woods and hears the voices from inside the wolf's belly, he cuts the wolf open and the young girl and old woman emerge. They fill the wolf's belly with stones, and while the wolf is still sleeping, stitch him back up. The wolf wakes and gives chase but as they try to cross the river, the wolf with the heavy stones dragging his body down, drowns.

•

I used to pick up rocks and write with a marker upon them something from my day
Climbed the Great Wall
Lay naked with Sarah
Felt little today
Talked with my sister
Saw the Flaming Lips at Crystal Ballroom

I would put a rock in my pocket, bring it home, write on it and then place it in a box or in a bag though sometimes I would forget about them and then discover my jacket or my backpack had all these stones sitting in them. When I left for Texas, I packed up all my rocks and brought them with me, and when my wife said I don't want to be married anymore and then left, I packed some of them up and brought them back with me to Portland.

Virginia Woolf filled her coat with stones and walked into the river. Her body was not found for three weeks.

•

The first of Jeff's shoes was first found floating in November of 2007. And the following May, the other shoe was found on the shore of Lake Travis, along with some bones of a foot. Almost two years after he had left. Nothing else was ever found.

Jeff, there is nothing that you are buried inside of or under. Only the inside of my body, only under my tongue.

•

Sometimes I just pick up rocks and write nothing on them. I just bring them home Jeff, and put them in the same boxes that hold photographs of your face.

•

She came home from New York on Thursday and wouldn't stay in the house. On Sunday she took a motorcycle ride with her friend's husband. His wife was in Oakland. The next weekend she took another ride with him, this time asking to borrow my leather jacket for sitting behind him on the back of the bike. They drove out of the city and through the hill country. Stayed out there until the following morning. She returned to pick me up to go to our first therapy session. It was late July in Texas and I could say that never had my body felt colder. But winter had been blowing through our home since the summer before. It had been so cold for so long, I didn't know what to say.

•

When Demosthenes had trouble speaking he was given stones to fill his mouth in order to still his stutter.

•

Sometimes everything is a rock. My wedding ring. Two stems of Craspedia saved from my boutonniere and her bouquet. The three of them together in a little jar. Sometimes feathers.

It is believed by some that the feather of the crow releases one from past beliefs. Outside my window is a large maple tree in which roost crows that wake me every warm morning. Sometimes when it is very early and they are very loud, I utter gently "please crows, not now. please, quiet" and their caws begin to stop.

My leather jacket I don't know if it fits me as well anymore. I don't know if it's due to my belly or due to her shoulders, or maybe something underneath me, that my body just cannot shake off of itself. Like invisible pockets in which I try to put my hands but there is already something in them.

•

Do my prayers reach you Jeff? Which star are you under? I keep lifting them, up out of the moss, to see what lays between them and the soil, and then put them in my pants.

•

I bring home any stone that speaks to me. Put it in my pocket
or my backpack and carry it home.
I moved back down south with bags and boxes of them.
I had a flowerpot full that I would move with me.
The flowerpot went with me from my house in Oregon, to her house in Texas, then to the house we shared, to the second house we shared, and then to the house I lived without her. Before I went back to the same house in Oregon I had moved out of five years prior, I picked out the special voiced stones, then brought the rest to the river and carried them down to the bank and beside the roots of a tree where I first held her, poured them into the water. Their bodies made a song of deep low sounds that flew upwards. The following day, as the airplane left Austin, my body made the same sound.

David picked five smooth stones and placed them on his person before going to face the giant. Only used the one. Hurled it at a god he was smaller than. The other four stones, David kept close, just in case there were other gods he needed to topple.

The birds dance trapped by the light that surrounds them. The birds flap frantic, touched by the light they sit inside of.

•

The god Cronus was the son of the Earth and the Sky. He was destined to be destroyed by his own son, and so with each new baby god born, he took their soft newness and ate it. When Zeus was born, his mother Rhea handed to Cronus a stone swaddled in cloth for him to swallow instead, and hid young Zeus away. When Zeus returned grown, he cut his father's belly open, freeing his siblings as well the stone that took his place. The stone he cast down to earth where it sat on a mountain.

Bound in chains by Zeus to a large stone in the Caucasus Mountains, Prometheus had his liver eaten out every day by an eagle. Every night it grew back, so the next day the torment happened again. This, for daring to bring fire from the heavens to the humans in the cold.

I think of the tiny skulls I tossed under the bridge. How the current always returns them to me. They keep talking to me, telling me to pick them up. To bring them home, to walk the world with my pockets bulging with their bodiless bones, the bowls that hold the holes that once held their eyes, to stitch my skin over them and swim to the island too far to throw a stone to.

•

Jeff, if I called you home and you came, in what form would you come to me in? Would you carry memory? Would you remember when we climbed into the car and drove into the midnight world to break into Barton Springs, how we got to its fence and with the chilled wind licking our ankles chickened out? Instead drove into the hills above. Winding through the dark and quiet suburban palaces, I saw a deer on a lawn. The grass was blue under the moon. Below us we could see the whole city, it looked like a jewelry box spilled. What a beautiful robbery.

On your far side of the father star, do you somehow carry the same vacancy that I do, the same decade of missing days that stretch the two of us? Do you remember, you and I? Making castles in the gray sand of Mercury's light? Do you recall the buckets of opals we drank down? The weight we wished to keep? Did you find it? The weight? To sink you down? Under the lake's surface? To keep you there what did you carry? In your hands? In your pockets? Do my prayers reach you where you are?

When you buried yourself under the water, you stole all my love with you. What a beautiful robbery. A beautiful heartbreak of robbery, taking my heart with you. I have been trying to grow it back over the years. Fall keeps coming.

It is possible to be wild and kind at the same time. It is possible to be both alone and be loved. I have known this to be true. In others. In me. To be loved. And to also still be alone.

Once, I found a beautiful woman with soft hands small enough to help me with such. But that is now gone. Like I said, fall keeps coming.

Once, the graves were made and marked with rough stones to keep the dead from rising. But I do not know what you are sleeping under. So I pick up any stone that calls. Just in case it is your voice calling from underneath, to release you.

Goat of my heart, everything in me you eat. Darkest wall of my brightest room. Yellowest tooth, biggest smile. The eyes of your stars still wink inside my night, so full I see them in the day. The flowers are beginning to pour themselves out of the branches. All the summers wait for you and your return to return. They will wait a long long time. I miss you. Sweet cherry king my youth is inexorably chained to from then to now and for forever, I miss you. The horses run, the trumpets wilt. The horses sleep, the trumpets shine.

•

It was said that Orpheus sung so beautifully, played the strings of his lyre so lovingly, that even the stones would gather themselves around him to listen and upon such, wept. That when the sole of Eurydice, the bard's bride, was bit by a serpent, Orpheus traveled to Hades and gained audience because of his voice. The king of the dead made a deal with Orpheus: the bard's love would follow behind him, back into the light of the living, but if the bard ever doubted such and turned to look upon Eurydice, the bard would lose his love. Ovid wrote how Orpheus, in the silence, began to doubt, and just before making it out of the underworld, he turns, to catch a glimpse of his love as Eurydice dissolves back into the shadows. Plato pens that there is no one following him from death, that the gods are but playing a joke on him, because they find Orpheus too much of a coward to kill himself and join his true love in the land of the dead.

•

I wonder if the stone that used Zeus used to save himself was the same stone he tied Prometheus to. If that which he used to save himself, he used in the punishing of another.

I went out on the lake you drowned yourself in. A tornado swept across it, whipped the water of the last thing that kissed your body into the air and against the boat we were forced to huddle inside of. I do not know where my wife was on that day. I don't know what month it was, but the sky hanging over the city you lived and died in was a grey mouth. Today is the same mouth that hangs over me. I aim for its teeth. When they fall, I pick them up and put them in my jeans. I bring them back home and put them under my pillow. Come morning, I lift my head to see what my loved ones—dressed up as gods as I slept—have left for me to sink my toothless gums into.

Eurydice

///

They never found you
—your body

and
            I ask again
                        closeness that was you—
            what rattled inside the flower your chest held so tightly
                        what shook it so terribly

and again
                        what rattled

                                                            what shook
            and again
                                                the rattling
                        and again
                                    what shook
                        and again
            and again
and again

it never stops   —and again

I ask
            again   was I
                              supposed to follow
                                          like Anne to Sylvia
                              you
                              to where you went
                        and bring you back
            bring your body   back   how
                              am I
                              still
supposed to
how
            do I follow
to where
                        did your body   Jeffrey

how
could you not hear
the size of the planet I whispered into your heart

I was so much louder then

///

All that surfaced were your feet
spread seven
months apart
both floating in
tennis shoes
in different pieces
of the lake

Even now ten years
gone and more
with
out you I
still stumble
online
for a lost report
to find
more news
hope some piece
of you
in some part
of a yard undug
will unearth

And just the other week I even
began
to hope
again
like I once did for those two years
after you had gone and before you were found
when I would imagine you
arriving
out of the lost world
and into the hearth of my arms
and wondered
would it be
less crazy
maybe

than you going
gone with no fare-
well no eyes to place
the crossing's fare upon
just a letter under
your parents' neighbor's door
slipped
before slipping
your open mouth under
the watery door on your own?

Or closer to crazy
to believe
that still
I might
still
hear a knock
upon my house
and open it still
to a man
with two feet gone
so desperate
to die and
yet not die
that he could
fling pieces
of his own body
far into a lake
and still
still
show up at my home
eleven years later
and still
with teeth
I would know in a snowstorm
know even were I blind?
Still? What more
who
more crazy?

Once I lost my brother
and it seems sometimes
still I am still
losing my brother still
every week
every hour again
and lord your sunlight
is so blinding today
Everything unseen in me
nobody knows and
nobody can see it
How do I possibly speak to any of it?

///

—to wanting to sink and letting the grass replace my heart and my
muscles replaced by the chewing of pigs, my body taken
by a breeze caressing the space it once contained

to the persimmon not being too bitter
            but without taste
to the branches
        not without wind but without the sound that comes
when it kisses them   to a day
not without light, but so much
and I am left to wonder
                                where is the shade to hold me
                    where the dark
            that gives me grace.

to the bees in my body making no sound but stinging nonetheless
to holding my heart under the faucet
and under the faucet
and under the faucet
        until I don't know if I am seeking to clean or to drown

to waking alone
to biking alone
to dinner alone taken
            quietly outside

to the leaves falling
            towards my food and clinging to my shoulder
        as if they are trying to say something, to me—

to the coming towards, the distance bridged, the drawing near—
to the arrival of the gentle things that approach my doorbell at dusk
—brows bare, velvet hats in hand, fingers stroking the brim nervously
            for gentle things are often nervous
                    when stepping towards animals in pain—and then waiting
to me letting them in
                so that

at least for a spell, little or large,
they can stand beside me, my arms hanging
            straight and useless at my side,
                              until I am ready to touch
                their soft limbs   and to let them
            touch mine in return   and to believe
mine are soft enough to deserve this

///

In the dark sand you lay and pour honey on your legs to feel a kiss
from the dark's creatures to feed their tiny bodies off yours
take their blood into their bellies to build their queen
out of your skin you felt them letting them bite you
it made you feel holy to burn   and to wipe the little things from
the top of your feet you were bones in a bag stood up
and breathed into to look more like a tree than bones in a bag
in some shadows you could pass for both fruit

almost

hanging   by its fingertips   from your crooked elbows
you bent   the hardness of their unripe skin under the iron
asked your grandmother to make them straight
she flipped you over like parchment paper
placed her broken english in your ear   it rattled
like a wasp's nest bouncing between your blue walls
unable to find space to stand the language of her body in
couldn't find its way back out
your other grandmother was just that   the other
grandmother smelling of cigarettes and a boring drive
to a house always lit the light of day passing
to stand like a birch twig not knowing
how   to be held   by those of the same blood
with different skin
you poured lime and milk into the dirt where you stood
you fought to keep the spirits in you and to keep
the spirits away unsure which ones
were the ones who wanted to hold you   you learned
to fight mirrors   the mirror fought back
    you taught yourself
how to draw a straight line with no ruler—
no castle wall   no country
                              claimed   vagabond
                                        flag
                    flapping
over the heart

a refugee
from nowhere
finding refuge in another nowhere—broke
every straight edge in the classroom grabbed
a fistful of two dirts   same color
       in different times of the dark   gave 'em both
names   of a country   built   inside your childhood
every time you cussed your mother
from behind a slammed door you left bruises
in your own mouth   broke your teeth
with stones   made angels   out of tea
leaves and tea
out of their wings
you still do not know
when you go into them
which rooms
stay and which ones empty
                              when the records came with beats bass
thumping against the windowless walls
their thickness
              reminding you
how thin you were   how not dark
you are
              which half
                          of the recipe
resembling what
                          most what   of you   you
              cautiously
stood
              in the doorways in place   running   man
                              your hands over your skin
until it was ~~smooth~~   enough
              to enter

29

///

after Jordan Edwards

Out of the soft and approaching night may we unfold our gentlest selves
coming to dusk with honey and mint in my mouth
something left behind their heart for me
to find on my walk today
tiny and purring

and at eve's soft hearkening upon my still knuckles
always a ghost of a sparrow finds the cups of my grace
or me a sparrow
in the ghost's cupped hands

last night at sunset and with the dead petals hugging the tires
it looked like the street was on fire

Saturday's flowers work hard for a living
they wait for me outside the front door every morning
even in the rain

and again
in the evening even in the dark

in the dream we were lions

and so none of that which was lion could eat us

and in another dream we were lions and that which was not lion
didn't hunt us
and in another dream we were lions and so beautiful

in all the dreams

and when we were awake too
even in the rain
and again in the evening
and again in the dark

Leda

///

In the beginning there was only the moonlight
and the rain

and the mud that was left once the rain had stopped
and the footprints left in the mud

made by my boots from when
outside in the rain I had stood

beside the gate through the whole storm
watching out into the nothing that was on the other side of the fence

and once the rain had passed and I had trudged indoors
dredging the mud across my floors and it was

only the moonlight and an inch of rainwater
collecting in my footprints in the yard and also

upon the thin bodies of the night blooming flowers
from out in the distance

the animals began
talking with the world

and I lay in my bed by the open window listening
to that world being born out there

and I watched the swans drop
from the dark air

to fold the lights of the night sky
into the down of their once soaring backs

and that's when you came home to find me upstairs
asleep

having tried so hard to stay awake but failing
and you woke me with what I know not

the harshest softness
or the most careful of violence

and your face was the first thing that I saw
in the familiar light of this new place

///

And with a breath pushed into my mouth by another—her lips pushed open
and against mine, open—we both became birthed. Both cobbled together in
much the same way. Built by ourselves the best way we knew how.

I thought I had dealt with what Jeff had wrought. Had written a poem
all on how grief leaves one eating and eating until then one's own self
is the only thing left to eat. And I thought I had then eaten it. And was done.
But my body was gone. And I kept trying to pick things up in my palms.
Twigs and pelts pulled out of the road. People and mud, the rain, leaves

all sculpted and smoothed best I could manage with the new hands I had
clumsily made for this new body, made out of mud and others, from leaves
held together with the rain, and the twigs, and the skins of animals still gone.

///

How hard the light enters the body. I put my hand against the glass
of the train's window, pushing to partway steady myself.
I am flooded by everything I see. A net tossed over the fish.
Hundreds of cattle in the field. The birds lifting together.
Around them is all that I carry

—the drives we would take
leaving Texas for Louisiana. Her mouth lowering into my lap
as we passed the refineries that burn in both.

In a quiet car parked on West Johanna Street she sang to me
...like I learned to love the bomb...
I can still see her turned towards my stare—looking me in the eyes
stripping her fears to share with mine while the blue Texas night listened
outside the window and leaning in
as her voice sung through its soft singing.

•

I could write a book I tell you. On the ways that I have known her.
Of the days that she loved me soft and true.
And she would probably say it was all just whatever.
That none of it was. True. Or else why
would she have inhaled the bodies of others?
How else would we be here? But it was.
True. Though we are. Though she did. Over and again. Many times.

There were the years before when she would call me *baby*
with the gentlest hunger. How it always made me smile.

And before all those times—the first time I held her unclothed shoulders
in my arms, she cried from how wet her heart was
after holding my face to her lips.

I cannot unremember this.

Nor how when we would travel north to her family's home she would call
from the far side of the house for her mother and call her *Mama*.

And how in the little house on East 3rd
where we first lived together and slept beneath the blanket taken
from her grandmother's home, she couldn't let me leave a room
without first kissing her.

///

We had taken Zepplin out to the nearby baseball field
so he could chase birds to his heart's content.
We had spent the night moving our two skins into one
until the sun rose and then went to the nearby diner
patroned by old men and served by old women to eat eggs and toast and
then under the early morning gray light
walked back to the house at the top of the curving hill
and fucked again before falling asleep
and then waking in the late afternoon to take the dog for a walk.

Beside the diamond was an electric box covered in bees,
all of them consumed with the hum of the metal,
loving its surface with their bodies.
While Zepp wandered the scents through the forest
we took turns practicing jump rope with his leash,
excavated our hearts to share silly walks with one another,
made up songs on the spot, unafraid to look wrong to the other.
When Zepp came bounding out of the trees
literally tumbling down the hill
a scream in the air coming from out the bunny in his jaws
we grabbed him by the scruff of his neck
made him drop it but didn't know what to do
with the rabbit's dying but not yet dead young and torn body.
Neither of us could start our morning with killing something
so we leashed the dog and leaving it behind us, walked for home
our hearts shaking, holding each other's hand.

Years later, one of her affairs was with a man who knows how to quarter a
deer. He was neither the first nor the only.
But he knew how to put up a wall and take apart
the engine of a motorcycle. Knew how to play the piano.
He who was married to my wife's closest friend in Texas.
He who that summer would sit down across the table
time and time again to share brisket with me.
He who visited her in my hometown, stayed
less than two miles from my parents, slept with her
in the same house that she and I had slept in years prior

the night before we flew off to our honeymoon. Who
when he left his wife for mine
took their copies of my books with him.

He knew how to shoot and how to cut the throat
of a quivering animal, skin it once dead,
and who if needed to
could probably pull a rabbit
out of a hound dog's mouth
and for the rabbit's own good
step down on its wet neck. Something
neither I nor her
were able to do.

///

Everything is a house that birds fly into and die

my mother and I box up the wedding plates
that were left for me

looking at the wedding bouquet on top of the bookshelf
I are surprised at what my wife did not take with her
and what she did

      her wedding dress
      the wedding photo her mother had framed
      the cast iron skillet gifted from my friend Shanny

I stare into the uncomfortable
and approaching future that takes the cloth
and leaves the leaves of the branches

everything in my body is falling acorn even after having hitten the earth

how the gods listen when you are young
and then one day both of you stop to what is being said and heard

before she left she made me take down the lights and board all
but one of this house's windows
before she left she made me take down the lights and board all
the house's windows but one
then threw its shutters open to draw the grackles indoors

used 18 months to teach me how to learn
how to sleep amongst the loud
and hollow bodies

///

The last time.
She had headed to bed
in the other bedroom as sometimes
she had trouble sleeping beside another body
and this was after she had let go of whatever peace
that sleeping beside mine had once brought
and she needed sleep that night
and I was leaving in the morning for two weeks in Shanghai
and from our bedroom I heard her call for me
from the other bed and ask if I would lay with her for a little bit
that she didn't want to be kissed but would I
lay next to her and maybe hold her
and how gently happy my heart then felt
even under those months of dark clouds and said of course
and climbed in beside her and she put my arm around her back
and nestled into my neck and chest as she once had
so often and there we lay
until she burrowed further
into my arms and began
kissing me and I began kissing her in return
and at some point some of our clothes came off
and her hands moved over my skin
and it had been so long since her love had touched me
in the way that it had when she had once let her being love me
in the way her heart did and yet
it all now feels like it was something like
putting in autumn dry soil into cups for the seedlings
and uncertain if any would break through after winter
like trusting in something only because once
we did—as if what we held in our hands
could be tasted by lifting it to our eyes
instead of tasting that which was
already sitting in our closed mouths
like having already ordered and the food arriving
after the hunger has passed
but still you both sit there

40

finally lifting the spoon
to sip at the soup though
since having gone cold now
saying *What is that, rosemary?*
Yes, I think so. And perhaps basil?
Yes. Here's a whole leaf.

///

Those early mornings
cutting up the cucumbers to send with you
into the gold world that broke across our driveway every a.m.
with Texas waking up on our street
and while the buildings burned like clocks
upon our front step I stood in my underwear
in the shadow of the radio the fragility
of daylight on my bare legs
watching you from our door
as you got into your car to go to work
the lunch I freshly made for you in your hands
your kiss on my lips and me wondering
how to save any of this warmth on my cheek
any of the candlelight on my tongue
this ancient Greece-erected marble that sits
beside the collection of hearts inside my heart
        —O sun
—you are dying
while many crazy men sit on thrones
pressing thumbs to forefingers over every lit match
and everything the jackals do pull the body out of my life
I never knew how to carry a dead animal indoors
without wrapping myself under its weight
no one teaches you what to do
when something that loves you still goes away
and leaves you to learn how to find something to love
that is larger than their absence
those mornings early in our marriage I would cut
objects that were once growing
to package into your Tupperware
slice a banana with berries and juice
to feed you breakfast
believing I had long since pyred my love
for the best friend who buried himself
those mornings when I had not yet arrived
at your leaving and his resurfacing
I would stand in the timid light of our kitchen

with a carrot and a green pepper
and the knife in my hand would not tremble in this dance
I am so used to all the funerals and all the radios talking
I hear I have been made excellent
at doing other things
while still listening for death

///

only the moon knows you and I when it was just you and I
how long does it take for a toxin to truly leave the body and leave the heart?
even my shadow aches even now I want
the serpent that coiled between her legs tucked under the petals
even this a poem that when inside me saw the light of my mother
and walked towards such ended up at the dark
touch of the outside world that keeps on leading to her
harpy martyring herself under her own claws
all meat I eat is spread with the dust of a dark country I almost entered

I have been neck deep inside the creature's speckled and curving belly
how wet my pupils were—even after
I sucked from the bite marks to taste the ways I had once been touched
I do not deal in metaphor I only write what is\
if the poet says the knife is a snake it is not *like* a snake it is a snake
if I say I am bag of Georgia twilight, it is because inside me the cicadas lift
I say every other day I convinced myself not to leave earth
we all sometimes swim in the dark part of the sea
sometimes it is not the sea but the swim back that pulls us under

my mother telling me of the time she tried to die and the stars threw her back
my mother the reason I have not finished myself
my sister
my father simple with his love and trying only to serve
the faces of Jeffrey's parents years after the funeral
no rain only petals of soft yellow warmth falling out of the air
my heart utterly imperfect and beautiful
the lightest feather on the back is also the largest stone in the sack
the part in the track where your head stops nodding and your blood starts?

44

I wish a bell of a distant place to sing and remove all that lays inside my halls
I wish a strange laughed redhead with hipbones
a red carnation waits under the plate and the plate is heavy
I pray for weight
I pray for hunger
the body an aviary built of small birds and the large spaces between them
a dead bird trapped under the skin of my left shoulder
and a live one hurricaning inside the right
I am still a stone lion yawning at the dawn

take your birds
I tire of scraping them in the dirt behind me town to town
people pay me too much for the fowl I kill that look like themselves
my poems are simply me practicing myself
my exterior being decorated by its interior
and vice versa—I once was loved
and weren't we all even when we did not know it
even when we believed they had stopped
warm blood still pumped from something beneath the rock that one of us was
and the rock that one of us was becoming

///

Starting to cry as you jog through your neighborhood makes you feel like maybe your sadness is not real, like maybe it is something manufactured for a scene in a motion picture.

It also makes it difficult to breathe particularly when you might be a person who already has difficulty breathing. Sometimes I wonder if that is all of us. Wonder if that's what a person is—a thing that has difficulty breathing. I tell myself I do not work for sorrow, sorrow works for me.

Baby leopard to Mama leopard: Mama, what is that thing mumbling to itself?
Mama leopard: That is a person
Baby leopard: What is a person?
Mama leopard: A thing that has difficulty breathing

•

My wife has built me a canoe and put me in it. Has told me I need to row to the island in the center of the lake and that she will try to meet me there but she has to go in your own canoe and also that the canoe she has built for me has a leak in it. She tells me not to worry about the water pouring into the bottom of my boat. To just concentrate on my rowing and to let her concentrate on hers. As I head out she reminds me that on the island there may be monsters, wild beasts hungry to eat us—we just don't know! But the unknowingness of the future—what an adventure! I look behind me. My wife is sitting on the shore next to her canoe, not moving for the water at all. She pulls out a book and begins to slowly turn its pages, trying to keep the sun out of her eyes.

I do not work for sorrow sorrow works for me

•

As I run through the green and Texas streets
I mistake a distant man in a pink shirt for a deer
and wave at two tiny girls as I pass them.
They may have actually been sugar snap peas, there is not much I can trust
these days, least of all myself. There must be some part of my youth still
blazing somewhere inside of me.

46

Two nights ago when biking with Mandi past the people dining outside on East 11th I yelled GOOD EVENING in a spirited yet sophisticated manner. It was a cannon being fired from some distant life I once wore, it felt like me.

I can see me on the other side of a large gorge, waving. Even from this distance I can see he has pretty hands. I wave back but not quite sure what it is I am waving

I do not work for sorrow sorrow works for me

•

I wish that me was a bigger me. I wish it enveloped the me I am right now. I am so small right now I do not know why it cannot. For the first time in more than a decade I am my college weight. This is not a good thing. I am skin draped over sharp wind.
I want to talk to the world.

The curse of the internet is that this desire is fed. But you are also made to believe you want what the world has to give back, even though you don't. Even though you do. Even though you don't. The world can give nothing back to you.

You can only give your self to yourself. And/or give your self to another self. And be fine or not fine with this. This is not always under one's control.

I do not work for sorrow sorrow works for me

•

There is an ocean of sorrow in all of us.
I have tried to learn how to spend my days not swimming in it. To stand on its shore. To only tip my toes in its water once in awhile.
And should I take a dip, shake its drops from my shoulders and leave. This does not always work.
And when it does there is still sometimes a breeze blowing from off its salty waves, pushing through the air to find me. Sometimes people visit the ocean in me and send postcards.
Hello Anis

We are at your ocean of sorrow
Thinking of you!
I try not to write back

This past year I have been treading water.

·

When I was a boy there was an episode of *Magnum P.I.* where he had to
tread water in the ocean, waiting for some boat to rescue him. It's the only
episode of the show I truly remember. It would flashback to when he was
a boy, practicing treading water with his father, and the hour length of the
show is the longest he has ever done it for.
I have been treading water for a year.
There must be some part of me still young.

I do not work for sorrow sorrow works for me

·

I am no king of clouds. Have never had this need to clutch so tightly these
bolts of thunder. No need to sit upon these patterns of weather, looking
down upon the earth below my feet, searching for something soft to
throw against something hard. More so quick-footed and ankle-winged.
Sleeping under sheepskin. Carving turtles into lyres. And holding the
hands of those traveling to the next world. We are all traveling to the next
world. I can only give my self to another self and be fine with this. I do not
know if I know how to do that anymore. Being fine with this.

How does one work with sorrow while not eventually working for it?
Does Hermes work with death or for death?
All the people I see are deers. I keep my distance.
Wait for them to pass, or to become people again.

Borus, Notus, Zephyrus. And Eurus

///

Jeffrey
I can no longer remember your bedroom

I don't know
in which of the caves in my skull
it is

You were the sound of crickets keeping me up in the night
the songs the world sang through
the green legs of its little children

I wonder how you did it
what you weighed yourself down with
when you went into the water
did you tie anything around your ankle
wear a coat of stones
or maybe just clutched them in your fists

Were you conscious in the last moments
or did you drug yourself
just before going in

These things I will never know
—the weight of your child in my arms
the names you would have given
to her and to the ones who followed
the leading of them into the corner of your house
giggling to tell their ears
the secrets of their crazy father
and the stories of what he was like
when he was young

•

You wrote a poem
you did yes
I can no longer see the words but

I saw it
when you lifted your head and the light touched you
first upon your cheekbone and then again when your face kept
lifting itself skyward
your neck

•

In a dream he comes to me
and says *I am sorry*
but I had to go
Anis there was a lion
and the lion was eating me

•

Say
they had found more of you than just your shoes and your feet
not even your whole body but say
even just your legs and if your legs were thick enough
would I keep one—that I might use you to hold my umbrellas
in the corner by my front door and to see every time I came home— and
if so would I then get not only one umbrella but enough
to constitute keeping you close enough to carry a collection
of things that keep me dry in this world

Or maybe if your leg is just the size it is
or as there is no longer is when it comes to you—*was*—
if your legs were the size they were the spring I saw you last
—in the parking lot of *Star Seeds* the diner down in Austin
off I-35 at Southeast 31st where you bellowed the last words I heard your
voice yell in this world *you still my boy!*
and in which your legs were the same thinness they had been since our
freshman science class when we first met—would I then just hollow one out
so it could hold say only one
very thin umbrella

Or a walking stick perhaps

Or better yet
a long skinny precious sword

that I could use to open letters
every time one arrived from the kingdom of the dead
bearing your garbled and scrawled name across it
written as if spoken with a mouth full of rocks

I would recognize it in any alphabet
and because I have missed your stories so much these last ten years
I would long to read in my home
about where you have been traveling ever since you left this place

•

How long can the human heart live
out there on the boats
when no one comes
when one is alone
and one stays alone because no one comes

How long does the human heart live

out there
                        on

out there   there   are

boats

and n o one came
                        to you

I never came to you

I suppose then the answer is 29 years

•

I had no idea how much frost had come
it was only after I started to thaw
from a winter different from the one you left me in
that I begin to see
how much water I am made of

and even in winter so much of me a river
like the one you and I both grew up beside
you on one side of it and me on the other
sort of like how it is now
you on that side of it and me on this one
how it is once again
how it will always be

•

In some world of these worlds that we do and do not traverse
my atoms and your atoms move together
in the same space of the same body
or because I do not know what happens
to the body to the spirit to the science when a person kills themself maybe
you and I already are
in some world
you

and I

are
maybe married in some strange but perfect marriage
perhaps how a tree is married to an earth
and how the branch married to the fig

instead of how the fig is married to hunger

or how a tree is married to a sky

///

And if the tree is on a hill
where one can sit
beneath its skyward embrace

and if the sky can be seen
between the tree's many fingers

and if the tree provides
the silencing without quiet
that all our bodies need

and if the tree
has fruit of which one can pick
and one does
and in thank you
touches one's fingers to the trunk of the tree

and if the one is not the only one
but many and several
who come and sit under
and sip of the tree's shade
and drink of the cool
breeze that gathers around the tree's shoulders
and if one pulls
the soft weight of fruit
from its thin branches
or lifts the golden to orange orbs
off the ground
from the tree having
dropped them there as if to say
here
take these
have
what I have to offer you
that which I want to give
is so heavy I cannot hold it anymore
but instead must set it here
for another to pick up

and if one loves the tree
even if maybe one has but only come once
to sit and watch the world
from under its leaves and then leaves
with not even realizing
how much gentler one's heart becomes
in the stirring
of itself after leaving
or if one comes for a regular spell
and so when in the neighborhood
when out for a walk
when on a drive through the old streets
and sees the familiar shape of the tree's silhouette and so gets out
and walks up to the trunk to smile
and then goes again
and if one comes
to trim the tree
and make sure that all its leaves
are getting the right amount of sun
and its arms enough water
and that there are no small things crawling
eating the roots
and if they are
guiding them elsewhere
as one may do if one does love the tree

and if the tree gives
not even for another
but because this giving
is what a tree does
and because this taking
is what humans do

and if the tree
is not a tree
but a cloud
no
a dog or a stone
a once god
hiding from that

which would make me into something else
or a beauty of which a god hid
inside the shape of a tree
to be kept
or maybe just a person
who maybe was once a boy
or a girl
or neither
or just a heart
wrapped in the trunk of a body
and tired
from watching
those who sit or feast or cry or rest or laugh beneath its shade
before getting up
to go into the day
with someone without their roots
so firmly planted in the years of earth
one who never had the good fortune
of being changed
into bark of sapling
and seed of sweet fruit
by hands large enough to clutch thunder
being changed into such
simply because some larger spirit or collection of constellations gathering
in the clouds
saw the skin of their love
as something too bright
to share with others
and so thought
here
I will place them here in this body
on this hill
in this sun
and starlight
that they may
do what they may do
and others can pass
and sit
and feast
and cry and

be heard
by themselves
and the tree
might be loved
for giving them this
and in their love
the tree might grow
to love itself

///

There was an old bra of yours in our chest of drawers
left behind once you were gone and for some reason
—I think perhaps as some last remnant of our intimacy

our closeness—I took it with me
but these years later it is forgotten
until I clean out my closet and then
once it surfaces I am remembered

of its presence and though I am done
keeping this thing of worn lace and covered wires
but still not knowing what to do with it say to myself *oh yes that,*
I need to put it with the clothes to go out

and then yet
somehow it keeps staying
being forgotten until it is being remembered

•

Do you remember
the night I put that bra of yours on   not this one but the black one   I do
we were in our room with a show playing that neither of us were watching
it was in the dark times when your body was still here but the touch gone

when your heart was still leaving but your body had not yet so
you both did not and did wish   to be touched   so maybe
it was your body that was leaving and it was your heart still remaining
—who knows   as that which we hold and that which holds us
often become one in any case—you

were laying on our bed and I
pulled the black bra on and filled it with shirts and pranced
a silly promenade swinging my hips to make you laugh
and woo you in the ways you once liked being
wooed by me with laughing the heart out loud
and in the way you once liked you laughed out loud

though you also too were already
feeling strange in being loved by me—
your laughter wrapped my body to yours
and then your hands
pushed me away again
and again this happened until
I pulled the bra off and sat
on the bed as well and you
still so unsure what to do
                    with your love of me
                    still warm somewhere
                    under the secrets of yours
                    that I didn't yet know were secrets
smiled a small smile
and frowned a small frown

back and forth and
back and forth between
my face and your magazine and back and forth between
your face and your shoulders between your eyes
and your mouth between your heart
and your body you fluttered

•

You once wrote my handsome husband you make me happier than a sunrise

That I have longed
for the body of one who once loved me like this
and then once became the executioner of that love
mistaking my heart for hers
my body for hers—
—that the last time I came across this old
once cream-colored brassiere I made a body from
a pillow to mimic her with the bra clipped
around it and laid with it under me—
is nothing to be ashamed of Anis

A plate of the darkest apricots was my love
soft and with wrinkles and
sweet and I wished so gently
to feed to you the darkest
and the sweetest of them

What is a little smile called—that which comes out despite
the best of the body's abilities to quiet the heart
becoming for but a moment before
already dusk
a day passing
made only of sundown and sunup
crossing between the purple and yellow shore
and the blue and orange one

not a smirk but a small dawn of a mouth
curving lightly
into that which is beholden to the trees darkening
while also turning
to a breathing
and gentle light approaching
a remembering
of what an earlier light had awakened before

Persephone

///

When they came upon the man with the large eyes and the mouth
open as the largest darkest well, he said to the travelers

it was not so much that I wanted to never think on her again
but merely wished to separate the echo from that which was echoing

everywhere I went I heard her voice—how it was when
she told me of her love how it was when she scraped me small

how it was when it was silent and saying nothing of the animals
she welcomed into our rooms the ones whose names I never learned

the ones whose names I did & who in the daylight after their shared darkness
she pushed me towards corralling me into friendships with them

unaware of their cowardice I welcomed their grins
when my loudness was caught on something else

there is a different sort of sickness that courses in killing the beast
and bringing it home claiming it was an accident and a different sort

of sickness to ask your lover to quarter it with the lights on
that you may have the pleasure of feeding it to him blindfolded

telling him it is one fruit when it is another
that the redness you drip on his chin is but blackberries salted

it is a different sort of sickness between the poisoning of a loved one and the act of
feeding the poison to them

and a different sort of sickness altogether
when pushing the loved one to feed the poison to themselves and then

once they do, when they go to kiss you, saying no
your mouth is full of blood

what a mess you make of everything you eat, can you not do anything right? I must leave, *leaving you to wonder*

where is it that I can go with this? with this knowledge? where?
I have had to make a Marrakesh of my heart

I have been making my way slowly but steadily to a fountain of birds quietly seeking red fruit the same size of my hands

///

In the country of dark rain I climb over your body
to find your body but all we both do is stare upwards.
Inside your body you and I are now only whispers

between the empty branches and Northern directions.
There are some days when yes I hate everyone.
Only my nephew is saved from this equation.

Perhaps too the stranger outside the window carrying
along with her box of books a mouth of sorrow.
Do you remember pushing the bumps of the lemon

over your lips? Fuck I loved you. More than any other.
More than anyone else. Where were you when we cooked
the same meat several times? Where were you

when like me the world worked at becoming softer?
Were you too late? Or too early? Or were you right on time.
And I was simply looking west, when you traveled from the west.

For some years I only read novels already read.
If I write the word read do you know if I will speak about
what is done or what is being? You will not. I do not know

the color of the seeds I throw until spring unfurls
her galloping hooves. Do not define the scent
of my children simply because I showed you

the interior of all my vases. I am allowed to lease
a studio apartment between the bang and the flash.
I could sleep on the couch for years without getting up

to answer the fires outside. I do not know sometimes how
to be the kindness I know my cursive spirit to be written in.
The longer I sit and write beside the large window
the larger my understanding often becomes. A path from behind
the dumpster back into the backlot wildflowers. Too many springtimes

carry too many names. My tongue is long enough to fit inside you

from many angles—all of them feel good. My first lover
pulled my lips with her mouth and teeth—I know of a map to stars.
Nights spent alone with the moon taught me how

I might use the body beautiful. Days in the company of the sun
learned me a language. The shovel my birthright. My body a birthmark
in the shape of a hole. One day my hands will open enough of the earth

to unearth the spade. Lust dustily telegraphs me every day.
I would like to roll your calves like a homemade Cuban cigar.
I hate the wasps she poured into my tea while calling me sugar.

If a woman of plush and promise were to see me naked
we are both made lucky. I believe in the Iliad of my skin.
Matisse, and girls wearing jeans. My skull

is marble and cloud. My naked hips polished.
I do not understand the hipness of cremation. Some part of my body   is
an urn and another part that which the urn holds.

But I find nothing organic about sitting for centuries. Fuck
I loved you and hated you. You may find me struggling to balance both on
the mantelpiece. I pray for earthquakes. I pray for the fireplace.

I pray everything that holds still. To break in half. For the floors
to be swallowed from below by some other country rising from underneath
giving out of its blackness the warmest rising loam.

///

The singer trapped in clay

The weight of dark birds in her veins

The rooster a poet seeing the sun before it appears from under the black earth

A voice that splits the bees became a voice that spilt them with intent

It is into our emptiness that the Lord pours his shape

There are a few times in a man's life when he is made completely of apples

A silver arrow carved out of a sapling

The broken husks of tractors becoming myth when buttoned up in moonlight

When I kissed the dirt on my wife's neck

The butterflies inside me make tremendous sounds until they leave my skull

Behold Anis—behind your back a gallop of mares canyons the sweet grass

When I turn I see only hills vaguely shaped like horses

Standing on the tip of the building hurling clumps of sod to the street

The lightning under her dress dances between my fingers

I dive beneath its folds to hold the tip of her electricity between my lips

Can smell the ozone of the storms moving on the outskirts of town

When they make love, wherever they are are trees

When we made love, wherever we were were trees

///

I have fists on fire. The flames are invisible. Everything I touch burns. What I pick up melts. If my hands brush upon something they singe its surface. No one can see this but me. What a god of destruction I am. My fists are invisibly punching through every window. On top of this world is an invisible world made of glass. Everything in that world is a window. Windows, people, small children, smaller dogs, everything is a window. And my fists are punching through all of them. Even though I am sitting quietly writing this in a public space. My fists on fire are singing through the glass souls of every person and thing around me. When my fists sing through the glass a bigger song is being sung. The glass song erupts into a block of birds birthing and dying over one another. People around me have no idea how clear and sharp they are in the invisible world. They have no idea the songs the invisible birds are screaming. They have no idea how much pain I am making. Having fists that constantly burn hurts. The people around me have no idea how much pain I am making out of my pain. I am invisibly drinking all the ways to die. Invisibly choking all small angels that invisibly sit inside me. In this world, the invisible world, I am a legend. The world trembles in front of me. I kill everything here and do not care. Nothing here can stop me from doing such. They cannot even see me.

In the invisible world my arms are held above me and being cut off. It is always the first moment of them starting to be cut off and the hour after it is done with me laying in the aftermath. In the invisible aftermath there is moonlight upon me and I am broken. In the invisible first moment the invisible sawing is about to commence and a scream is about to invisibly fall out of my invisible mouth. Far from the first moment and far from the aftermath is a ship on an ocean and I have no idea if either are invisible. But I know that I am on the ship heading towards a coast. On the coast is a tall thin house and in its tower a woman stands with a scarf around her. She is waiting to see the brow of the ship that carries me home. She stays up there through the night, and with sandwiches that she takes apart as you are prone to do and with a thermos of hot chocolate. She reads her book, she listens to a radio, she watches the clouds. When she catches the brow of my ship she will start to wave the scarf. Even in the red colors of dawn, her scarf stands out and I can see it. This is because it is dyed in the ink of her heart. It is so bright, made brighter by her love, which in turn is made brighter by my love, which in turn is made brighter by her love, and so on and so forth. I do not know if any of these things are in the invisible world. But they are not in this one.

///

North of the city we sat at sunset
Under the heavy iron hanging in the sky
Crushing its light upon the skull bones of the high flying flocks
And watched how the swifts flung their bodies
Away from the dusk and into the hearth
Of an abandoned chimney its bricks stuffed
With straw to hold warm at the end of summer
A puddle of ink spilling backwards into one point
A tornado dissolving itself into a place to sleep
Like the plug pulled and the drain swallowing them
Out of the clouds and leaving here for the land of the dead
On the hill in the grass of September your hand in mine
Your hand in mine your hand in mine your hand
I don't remember the dress you wore, only a blueness
And the warmth of your heart from pulling the blue off
The warmth of your hands on mine placing them to your breasts
A city of burning houses all the attic birds pouring out to drink of the eve
Your hand in mine your hand in mine a mine
To a fire under the skin not yet returning to a spark

///

The bride swings the Mexican piñata stick at the acorn shaped piñata and cracks the acorn wide open. Inside is a needlepoint bearing her initials and the groom's with a heart stitched between them and two wedding rings tightly threaded on to it. However, the rings loose their thin tethers, fly through the air and get lost in the grass, unbeknownst to the wedding guests who roar in excitement when the bride makes contact with the acorn. The piñata has been made specially for them by a shop in Austin, one of the ones that once dotted Chavez, and has traveled with them to New Orleans along with a piñata horse, colored a blue as bright as candy. The day begins with a poet from Ohio speaking like a southern gentleman, and continues with more poets, and then prayers from the groom's father and sister. Everyone is seated under a large oak, which minutes before, Derrick fails to loop a rope over to hoist the piñata up, which is the reason he had been holding the large crepe papered acorn while the bride and groom took turns swinging wild and blind at it.

After the bride breaks the acorn open, the groom's brother mouths to him the rings are missing and the groom in turn loudly announces to everyone *THE RINGS ARE MISSING*, in such a booming trying-to-keep-cool manner everyone believes he is joking. The groom pulls out of his pocket two porcelain bottlecaps, which the two newlyweds then pin to one another's breasts in front of the bride's great grandmother's quilt carried to the west coast from the Dakotas and then down south for the wedding. And while standing a hundred feet from a gazebo in Audubon Park where 43 years before, the groom's parents sat with cups of drugstore hot chocolate warming their hands and deciding to get married, the bride and groom kiss, as wife and husband, with her clutching his face in her two hands, cupping his cheeks that are flush with the tears that pour out too hard for him to speak his vows.

In the treeless grove where they have all gathered is a ring of a sidewalk circling the grass. At the start of the wedding, her father walked her down a part of it, as everyone sat with kazoos in their mouths, humming loudly *Here Comes the Bride*. And as soon as they are pronounced wed, the two of them take off sprinting hand in hand under the 100 degree day running a victory lap around the field. As their hearts pump and mouths laugh, he whispers to her *we gotta find those rings*. *What?* she says back. *The rings, they're actually missing* he tells her. As they round the home stretch, out of breath and beaming, Cristin, one of their dearests, snaps a picture of them glowing brighter than the sun, and they set out to look for the rings, eventually and surprisingly found in the grass by the bride's brother and one of the poets.

Later, he will draw a bath, both their mouths full of birdseed and their bodies worn from dancing. She will slide hers into the water, pulling him under with her, to wash the light from their limbs. He will kiss her belly and move his open lips between her legs, breathing his body through hers. In the morning, she will find that her overnight bag, packed by her sister, has nothing in it but cowboy boots, one skirt, and five books, so she will pull on one of his shirts, and they will walk towards breakfast, stopping to buy a toothbrush and toothpaste from the gas station at the corner of Magazine and Washington. The Sunday streets will be empty. They will stand over a sewer grate across from a cemetery and outside the fanciest restaurant in the city, and trade the toothbrush back and forth, spitting into the sewer grate while laughing in front of the restaurant's teal and white striped walls.

The day before, after the second piñata is burst, the children gather candy out of the blue broken horse, and hand the two of them a Muslin bag filled, with the sweets the kids do not want. Beside a vase of Craspedias, the two sign their new names. Watermelon sits on the tablecloth—so red, so bright—it looks like something fresh from the hunt, cut open and split wide to feast upon, its blood staining the teeth of everyone's smiles and running down all our chins.

///

I was a tree of figs
a bushel of dates picked plucked and dipped
in honey and rolled in oats

I waited days into months for something outside my body
to pluck the edible parts of me from the parts of me that grow them

My bodies grew plump
soaking up the sun making my thick skin under the afternoon light brown
into amber into gold and almost translucent

In the warm hands of the setting sun the snakes moved below me
the squirrels sought to eat me and they tore my flesh open
the seeds they couldn't fit in their cheeks they threw to the dirt

The snakes crawled above me
I clung to the underside of their bellies praying

That in the absence of wind that might have carried me
to the soft soil of the far fields—that the slither of their leather might
instead crawl me there with them

•

Do not let them tell you what in you you should grow
and what in you you should kill

They did not spend the years held by her hands
under the dirt for the purpose of her dark gardening
some were there as she did it
some of them watched

And when you halfway climbed were halfway torn from out the earth
and went to bathe the dirty from your arms and back only to find
the dirt was actually holes—actual pieces of your body now actually gone —
some of them wondered why you could not just clean yourself

There are strawberries upon the underside of the bed
growing—you scratch so hard
at and through the softness you rest upon
to pull their small bodies out from the cracks

For you too were once a small body falling upwards from others
had too once a grandmother and how so very much she loved you—
peeling oranges and grapes just to watch your very small mouth chew

Anis. May your heart like the moon grow
big and full
and in this absence of light
new

///

It was out in the orchard that we met the man in the white suit. His
jacket was folded next to him. He had an apple with him even though
the trees were thick with plums. He had a knife. Was lifting slices of
apple to his mouth with its blade. His hands were lighter than ours but
dirty. He saw me looking at them. Smiled and gave both me and brother
slices, said *There's a lot of dirt under my nails. All the unripe fruit that falls out
of the trees, it's my job to bury them. Get paid for every piece. So I watch the blue
jays, for when they alight upon the branches. And I send my blackbirds—I have
a flock of blackbirds—into the trees, and the birds thrash their bodies against each
other amongst the leaves, and the dark but unripe plums tumble towards the earth,
before they might fall on their own. I get paid for every piece. Would you boys like
a job? I've gathered so many blackbirds that sometimes I need help. As well as help
to gather and bury the fruit. You boys wanna help. I can pay you a nickel a plum,
it adds up.* We nodded, and at dusk returned to the same tree. We heard a
whistling. And then footsteps through the grass. And then the man in the
white suit walked up.

•

In the orchard, the man in white sends his blackbirds into the trees and
they shake the trees loose of whatever from their bodies is not held too
tight. The plums rain down and we feel the wind made by their bodies
passing before the thuds of them hitting the soft ground. *Quick* the man
yells. *Quick! It's best to bury them before they touch the earth, makes it easier!*
Me and brother run to catch the plums. The sun is far gone now, and
it's hard to see in the dark. But our eyes are young and sharp. We run
with our arms out. The not yet ripe bodies our embraces collect are so
dark—even inside the night that has now arrived, we can see this. And far
larger than any fruit we have touched. And in the light that arrives from
the stars, tiny and silent above us, they look much like brother and me. It
feels a little strange all this, but, we lift palmfuls of soil, and place the fruit
into the holes. Some of the fruit, they. They struggle. Like, they sorta
fight. Against being put in the holes. Which is weird but. It starts feeling
weirder, when there are pieces that didn't. And I swear they made sounds,
mostly what seems a kinda whimpering. I could swear I heard a scream
but brother says it was the blackbirds. Like I said it's all a little strange but
most of the strangeness passes. I just thought though that after we buried
them, they would stop making sounds

•

The man smiles, says good job. He's eating a piece of fruit, I'm guessing a plum this time, the inside of it's blacker than what an apple would be. I notice too his hands are cleaner than before. He calls his birds back in, like a fisherman pulling in nets, and keeps saying good job over and over. I don't even know if he's talking to us when he says it. One of the last ones we put in the ground, the man in white asked us to pause. He lifted the fruit back out, and sent us on to tend to the others. I heard him whisper, I don't know if for our benefit or his or for nothing, *I just want the thigh. Of the dark meat, the thigh is the softest part.* He never tells us what he gets paid for each piece, never told us who pays him.

///

While the moon was above and looking elsewhere, the men came in under the night. Took every flower in the yard, except one. They left it for the bees. And for the wind, to make laugh. For the sun to caress with invisible strands of hair. And for him, to turn over in his hands & for his fingers to brush his tenderness across. That he might be remembered of still having such, in the evenings of gentle ink, when everything becomes a river that flows nowhere. That he might have a soft lightness. Touching against his skin. A way to remember that a true going is also an arriving.

That he might, in the sitting of the dark water song of the night, submerged in that which is quiet and heavy and rising, have something light in his hands, that he might like a dirge rise with the river as well. And so this. The reason they leave him one. For these evenings—for that evening, for this evening—the men who come always leave one. While they carry the rest of summer's flowers stolen and slung in bags over their shoulders, wading the long water and threading the tall grass of the sunken meadow, to bring them to another place, just as others are on their journey, to bring the petals of a palace that sits on the other side of another mountain, to here.

///

Handclap in my blood
my sister's heart

pregnant with love
like our mother

always growing
flowers in the rain

how hard she has learned
to move easily through the world

when I dream my brother
I dream him always seven yrs old

there is a cossack in my chest
that sometimes drinks down his own sorrow

sometimes by himself
sometimes loudly

the cossack drowns himself
until the angel in him sings

there are stories
and then there is what is below

all that is light in me falls and thunders its way out
everything dark lightly approaches

held in my hands is a black bowl of warm black
I drink it happily alone

sometimes when others walk past
I still wonder if I may

sometimes when others walk past
I slurp louder that they might know of what I swallow

may my father be given the softest bed
may his most perfect music always sing his most perfect smile

the warmth of his gentle mouth may my mother always mother
may my mother always be

there are coffins in me built only from orange trees
may my graveyards learn from both

all the dogs in me talk through the moon
to the dogs in you

I have met young ones I wished were my daughters
may their always hearts always be

dark umbrellas turned inside out catching the sun
may we all stop breaking ourselves to hear our songs

may we all stop breaking others simply to have a sound to dance
to if my boat is body

the bow smiles back at where it once was
the stern seeks to see the approaching horizon

the hull of my heart filled
with dresses of silk for those who I have loved

when my body was a boat
what the boat of my body wished

was to carry itself home to my wife but she was gone
if my body is a boat

all it wishes is to hold all of me
over every sea and through every night

carrying bolts and bolts
of shining and yellow fabric magically spun

from out some distant land and journeyed back
to the place that has known my sound

if you see me walk past
with one shoulder higher than the other

under a sky so black it is blue
above an ocean so blue it is black

my starboard hand is trailing behind into one of the two
filling my left with stars

///

I suppose we all go treasoning sometime
Shooting the stork mistaking it for a dark lion
We should all be nice giants
With a rose on the toe of a black shoe
Waltzing without movement
Eating fruit from the source
Getting caught in the rain
Watching the world trying to
Write ourselves upon our bodies
Feeding the wolves alongside the saints
Everything is starving in some place
Under an orange night and holding a lightning rod but not any warmer
The moving world still as a Daguerreotype
Believing there is control to be had over wild birds
Uncaging the caged skylark even after uncaged and gone
Letting it go and still
Trying to unchop the tree I chopped down for you
My body has a dance caught under the skin fighting to smell the light
Freestyling with the promise of a meadow
Moving in the abandonment of self
Bicycle + night + the city = I dare you Anis to tell yourself you are not still alive
The holy mountain of the brain quieting
To be cradled by the spirit
Under the skin my stars itch
The leopard paces their kisses between the galaxy and my street
Dragging in the wet ghosts of my undead wife
To chase away the golden wedding I sought to lace over my needless shame
My heart of branches made bold and dark with the moon behind them
Collapsing suns and growing the leaves from under the old marble
Smoothing the inside of you Anis becoming
How far now my mouth from the lip of the urn
I wish to sip at the tip of a wetter prayer
Notice the soft fauna close by talking their bodies to the other bodies
Leave the cumbersome light to take them with me into the quivering

///

After the purpling of the apricots came
and during these cold days built of winter sun
I talk via letters punched into a phone with Jordan
on whose parents' floor the summer before starting college
I and Jeff woke upon one Sunday morning
after cramming our faces with the night before
scoops out of the 5 lb cheesecake he had made
in a round tin and had taken to make many
that whole summer long and then spent
that weird Sunday moving all day long
furniture for a stranger named Honey
New Orleans can be a strange city at times
and Jordan and I "talk"
about the interviews we recently have had
for a reality show about high school musicals
for life can be a strange city at times
and we talk about our production of the Wiz
both of us with one black parent
and neither of us looking such
and we talk about Jeff
—he being gone
and gone by his choice
or maybe not
as in—how much choice do we actually have
when the dark fisted flower grows inside the skull
until we must rent it out—
but that is a different poem—or not really
but it is—
SZA is in my ear singing
and Jordan then sends me a picture of her child
in her arms alive in this world only just this past month
new and with a middle name
named after that which comes back to us
out of the emptiness after we fall into it
and I ask her *is your heart full?*
and as I wait for my echo
to become her answer

my coffee cup is sipped
it is always full
either with coffee
or with emptiness or some ratio of both
and I put another SZA song on
and Jordan returns
with a yes of enthusiasm today
on the longest night of the year
—*Shabe Yalda*—
and as my family is in another state and my father
no longer a boy in Iran
shortly I will go buy a watermelon to slice and a pomegranate
to break underwater with non-Persians while we trade
records off the needle and smiles off our hearts
and tomorrow we—all the We—will have made it
out from under the gaze of heaven's evil twin and only
by doing what humans forget we do best—gathering
together in dark
to laugh, to eat, splitting
sweet fruits given to us by this earth
that loves us still in spite
of that which we forget—
that of which what we do best
gathering inside one another
so that we might
from under the longness
that will always come—
come back out

Prometheus

///

I was in a car and had arrived at a beach of stones. And all the stones were skulls. And I knew the skulls. In a different life I had skinned the animals from them. Would shoot the animals, cut their cloaks from their bodies, clean and boil the bones. I filled my house with the skulls. And they would talk to me as I tried to sleep. Until I could no longer live with so many of death's marbles. So I carried them to the sea and threw them all in and in the sunlight of the afternoon I returned home and opened all the windows and doors and slept peacefully on the floors, empty but for the moon having softly entered and still so slowly approaching.

In a distant castle I was a fool dancing before the throne in the early evening. And on the day of battle I would find myself singing into the giant pots hinged on the walls, the oil boiling inside them. When the armies would charge I would turn the oil onto their shoulders, I would watch their eyes turn into holes, the lips become fat dripping off the scream. This was my job, turning souls into steam, except no armies ever came. The castle was empty. I would dance before empty seats in a silent throne room, convinced that something I could make laugh and in return would make me feel holy, would one day come to fill the chairs.

When the white man laughed over the body of who he called Indian and then acted confused when his head was hunted in return, I was the sound of the hard earth kissing the legs of running animals. The thunder I was, thundered without lightning nor storm. When there were no animals I waited. There were never any animals. The America of me was only men wandering lost through the plains, sitting in the dirt and watching for the clouds to bring something to them—men made bloody as red and men who were white like ghosts and men who were black from being pulled out of the earth. So many men white and like paper losing themselves when it began to rain. So much wind came down out of the sky and carried the paper bones somewhere where they could not collect themselves together. So many men not made of paper turned into bright and dark flowers, because they were not paper, and could be picked, plucked, and opened. So many men called red because of the bleeding. So many men called black because of the holes placed across their bodies.

There is a jukebox up in the mountains. It plays and calls for me to climb to it and to carry it back down. And once I do it sings for me to carry it back to its place adjacent to the clouds. All lifelong I bring it back up the mountains and all life long I am bringing it back to the earths. I do not know what it is I wish to be. A prayer, or one who prays. Listening to the songs I carry like well water back and forth. Prometheus. Sisyphus. Prometheus. Sisyphus.

There is a rap song made of only a bassline which when heard all that you are will become hyacinth. It is playing in a car somewhere, conquering the street, turning the drivers and the whole strip, the whole town into a cold field of color, blooming and dying once a year on repeat. There have always been these wet fields, and always children running through them. So often, that the children when they grew up made their houses there and made their children there and their children kept laying in the wet red fields making angels out of the lines of their bodies, and the makers of the makers of the rap song—that wasn't so much a song as it was a dark throbbing sound humming low and deep like a whip cracking slowly through centuries—pointed deaf to the cracks and said look, look at what you keep making with what we have given to you, wet red angels, you must love making your bodies into dead flowers, this must be what you want, for you keep making homes out of this wet red sinking field we keep building houses upon. Prometheus. Sisyphus.

When the marquis landed from Spain to the new valley, he burned his men's boulders, to keep them from being chained to the mountain they had avalanched out of. When I was a conquistador I dreamt of a skyscraper, a thousand stories tall, that was on fire. My wife was in it, hanging out a window on the top floor. I climbed the metal walls, all thousand stories I climbed to save her. I took her in my arms and climbed us to the roof. Where she asked me what did I expect us to climb down on. I stared at the flames howling up at us. I stared so hard they shrunk. I stared so hard into the clouds, a thick rain came and drenched us all. My wife said I *can still smell the burning the burning is all I can smell.* I woke from this dream, and did not know what a skyscraper was, did not have a wife. But I saved my wife. But I did not have a wife. But I saved my wife. But I do not have a wife. There is a space in my bed from something that was once something. I woke feeling heat on my arms, rain on my shoulders, and a fat house of fire still burning in my heart. And locked inside the burning house a woman as beautiful as the ocean when calm, laying asleep in my arms. And at her feet, my love clothed in a skin of soft fur, a jaguar purring in its dreaming. I did not know how to wake it, to have it open its eyes, cannot tell you how much I long to know their color.

Before I was becoming a conquistador, I was but an archer aiming my arms at a white hole in the sky. I was not dark as the sky but brown as the ground and another boy who was white like the hole told me the hole was the moon and when he held a mirror up to his face and told me to look in it, I saw a reflection of his face staring back at me. When he took the mirror down, I saw a reflection of my face looking back at me. After he told me it was moon and showed me how his heart was my heart, his skin my skin, he kissed me on both, and turned himself into a rabbit. I watched while the rabbit peeled the pelt from his muscle using his own teeth. All that was left was the night, and the sun's white echo, and rabbit's skin. My skin. I pulled rabbit over my shoulders, slept and woke with his blood on my shoulders, and as the blood dried into a dense new body I broke all my arrows, convinced myself I could use my wicker quiver for drinking water. Sat at the river, filled it and sipped. So thirsty I couldn't be quenched. So thirsty I could not notice my water falling from woven grass into unwoven grass. I kept drinking and missing. And drinking. And missing. Around my shinbones flowers sprung forth, thirsty as I was, for the rain my body gave.

I do not know how I found this beach. But here I am in this place with these bones I once knew washed up on the shore. There must be a map sewn into my heart that always leads me back to the work that was done by my body in other ages. I think of the skulls I threw over the bridge. How the current has always returned them to me. And how I have carried them to others and then back to the sea. And back to the others, and back to the sea. How full my arms are. How full my arms are. How tired my arms are. How tired I am and still how these stones once used for breathing need to be washed in the salt, and in the water, and in the time that moves them both.

///

Some summers past I sat on the stairs to the basement
with the woman I loved. It was hot outside—
August in Portland—with no air conditioning and we had popsicles.
She had driven from out of town to surprise me as I flew into home.
Stood by the airport gate in the dress she had worn on our first date
fabric the color of tangerine peels and with long yellow flowers in her hands.

On that hot day we sat in a cold movie theater and watched
half of a bad movie before stepping back into the heavy sun
and laughed on the walk home marveling at how loud the hearts
of the trees were above us and made love in my bed our bodies moving
like the breasts of sleeping birds slowly and quietly our skin
clinging together in the sweat and heat until finished
and then trying to let the still air cool us down lay next to one another
and smiling before getting up to go down
to that basement to eat those popsicles.

Some years later in May she married me. It was hot that day too
—after officiating the wedding Derrick walked the streets of New Orleans
with his black shirt in his hand searching for a cold bar.
Some years after that hot day she stopped being married to me
but didn't really let me know. It was a hot day in North Carolina
and I wasn't there and someone else was. And on a hot day in August
she did finally tell me she was done and left and I swallowed Texas
eating barbecue with people who love me.

It is springtime in Portland as I write this. Sleeping the nights while here
in that same basement. It is hot outside this week and cool underground.
Earlier today me and Adam ate breakfast together
and sat and talked until it was time to eat again, so we did,
and talked until it was time to eat ice cream, so we did.
And on the way there I noted a tall skinny house I liked
and stopped to take a picture of a small hill of blossoms the house sat upon
petals orange as my once-wife's dress.

Adam and I have been friends for almost two decades.
And with a little more than two years before we both turn 40

we sat in a shop on Division beside an open window and ate ice cream
while the sun licked our arms and a girl with horse tattoos
sat on the bench outside—a horse head on her shoulder,
a leg and hoof on her calf.

I thought of Chris, a day or two before saying as we played
a lawn game from the afternoon into twilight, all of us sleeping afterwards
in the same house on the Oregon coast for the weekend
as we had done the year before and had done the six years before that
long before I ever even knew the woman I once wed—
him saying this is a good life. A good life.

Wiping the coffee ice cream out of my beard
I told Adam what Chris had told to me
and we both agreed.

///

Perhaps in whatever place we travel to when we go
from here to there which comes next perhaps those
and that of who we knew when we moved through
this blinking being we know as our lives right now
are the world itself we arrive in. A planet made out
of those who held our hearts and out of the hearts
that were held by us. A planet made from once was
and what might have been. Our winters our autumns.
The summer months. A band of shirtless and brown
children running through the light of those months.
The electrical farm, the middle name of the postman.
The maiden dancing alone and the dance she dances.
The starlings gathering to take from our giving hands.
All that we once loved and that which once loved us.

Grandfathers we never knew. Oak brown rivers now
the color of green apples washed in the sunlight made
now of a grandmother gone before grown. The house
in Iran my father as a boy sung to himself inside of now
the grass under my bare feet. My father at 6 a caterpillar
inching across the blades. The grass soft as the horses
roaming them, soft-haired wild and calm—and the part
of my father's mother she never let loose in the life she
fed me in. The rice she spooned on to my plate, amber
hairs in their manes, their hooves my childhood dishes.

My mother 8 years old and whistling with a book back
in Mississippi, now the wind touching my neck, and her
fingers moving along my ear as she did when I was once
small enough to be bathed. My mother a wind carrying
pieces of the sea, the sea my sister, a song of many lands
sung in the water. My sister the sea's song and a glassless
window and also a spyglass on a tripod looking out and
across herself to the land on the far side of herself—my
nephew, this countryside she gazes at. The white cresting
waves she lifts to lay upon him, my nephew's teeth. And
where my sister changes colors in the water, to become

an ocean—the love once swirling between my wife and I. Inside her, I see yet again the brown and shirtless children splashing. In her water. In the delta. And in spring.

And the spring. And the spring. The spring.

When I get there Jeff may you be in season your blossoms full in bloom. May the trees be tall and may I gently lay beneath your leaves. The pink petals of what you now are drifting down towards the open mouth of that which in this world I knew and named as my heart, happy to be touched once more by the warmest time of the year.

///

Friday night. Cleaning the hallway closet. Making beats.
And biking to bookshops to listen for the wind of its books.
To the night as we pass through one another. My kingdom
for a castle of purpose. My kingdom for another kingdom.
Saturday morning at the turrets. Flew flags. Wrote poems.
Ate sandwiches at the butcher's. Company of a sweet lady
and her wild daughter. Sat at a place called Poet's Beach.
It's on the gray part of the river. Under an overpass. Rocks
pushed out of the dirt to make a space. Like all good poets.
Went wading in the wet mud. Read Mark Strand and Robert
Bly into hair of a person I would like to bury my body under.
Jumped skinless off the dock with one of my other brothers.
Caught a child when she jumped too. Watched as a fountain
erupted with children not yet folded over by the low departure
of childhood. Took a bite of a four year old's ice cream. Stuck
in my teeth I had sprinkles of a rainbow. Ate pie on the lawn.
A slice we sliced three ways and the blackberries fat. Then
showered and lay in bed I was alone and unclothed reading
Roger Reeves and falling asleep beneath a stack of Archie
comics. I woke. And from the window of my staircase saw
moon behind the black fir bright as frozen lakes under blue
night. And waking with a hunger breaking, ate cantaloupe
crisp and with blueberries and root beer I sat above the black.
Felt myself continue on its watery quest to become paper.
Been two years now since clutching the rags my sprung heart
down in Texas had been torn into and terrified to leave but
more terrified of dying so with two best friends I broke bread
and flew north, Been at the loom ever since. Knees in dirt.
Neck in dirt. A body whose flowers I couldn't really tell you
the colors of. Different shades under different days. Different
colors in different parts of the dark yard. And each day a day
when a black body in the dirt is made again into bright light.
Circling us a ring of bodies killed for their darkness and youth.
In spite of such I stay threading. Or rather because of. Weaving
beautiful on the quietest of weekends. Unsure how to start I only
seem to fear endings for the dread of a new beginning. Hands that
once offered themselves open saying: *place that which has been*

tired of traveling softly here.   I wish my heart. To make sense.
A smile from flowers. A creaking from weight stepping on the ice.
As it has at times. Some days I want the morning and to be shared.
In the way I might be shared with one who has traveled the same
hills of sleep journeyed while laying beside another body through
the night. To once more have another call me by my other name
of home. Or for at least the wanting of the wrist of another. So
maybe all I wish is the want. Yet without the longing.

                                                        Ish say
Sunday is my rope.
And when waking today to light different than August
and with different light than July and Septembers past,
waking to a different bird than the crows who I swear
know my voice—I hear the truck across my street that
has sat silent and unmoving for more than a year now
its sides caked with the dirt of 16 months stillness and
of which just last night I said to another softness man I
wonder if the truck runs & if its owner would sell and I
having never heard its voice before this morning hear it
sputter—hood up like the way we wore ours all spring
the year Trayvon was killed—and trying to start again

///

In winter I would lie
in the garden and sometimes pretend I was something other than myself

A carrot
A rabbit
An echo of something bigger than the shade over my heart

Sometimes in the garden
night would arrive
holding cupped in its hands the moon soft cheeked and full
glowing like the face of an orange skinned woman in a more orange dress

and the enormous night would use the moon to tell me *you are like how I
am and see how bright my body sometimes becomes*

In the garden I waited for spring
Always I waited for spring
And for my love
to appear like it

returning

out of the cold
and with flowers upon its fingertips

///

And when spring arrived I
took a class to learn something
I had never before learned
and a thing I thought I might love

How did we make it
through this winter?
after the year we had?
And while knowing what awaited us in the new one?

How amazing we
who have stayed
are   how beautiful and heavy and
vulnerable we who couldn't were   oh

—when spring arrived I learned how to carve from wood
a large spoon! I hadn't ever done that before
and I haven't done it again since
yet   But I learned it

As I have learned more
how to hold my heart again
and whisper into it
and once more listen

a little better
to the songs it sings
even mouthless with
no mouth it sings

and even when no note
heard nor even made
I am listening or at least learning
to always try to

so perhaps it is not
the longest night we at times find ourselves in
but simply the slowest dew
forming upon us

///
Acknowledgements

Thank you to the editors of the following journals in which some of this book's poems first appeared, sometimes with different titles or in different forms:

Buzzfeed Reader, "The plums"
Gamma, "Translation"
Drunk In A Midnight Choir, "The flower"
The Paddle Wheeler, "Some summers past"
PDX Monthly, "Underworld" (originally titled "Mine Shaft")
The Harpoon Review, "Leda" (orig. The swans)
Thrush, "5 months"
Used Furniture Review, "The astronomy of this thing"
Nailed, "Proserpina" (originally titled "UNDER MS FREY'S ARROWS I RETURN TO THE POETIC STACKING OF PICTURES I FELL IN LOVE WITH INSIDE OF MR McDANIEL'S HANDS")

•

In the poem "Some sort of funeral", the line "that you had to go live once again back with the animals" is directly inspired from the Moonface lyric "and now you live back with the anglophones", from his song "City Wrecker". The poem "Pacifics" draws its title and the line "Sunday is my rope", from the Digable Planets song Pacific Heights (Sdtrk 'N.Y. is Red Hot')".

•

If you are feeling helpless or alone, first, know that that is alright and completely human, and that there are so many of us who feel that same way, myself too at times. Second, talk about what you are feeling with another person, especially if there is the thought, idea, or want to harm yourself or another. There is no shame is speaking on this, and that conversation is important for creating a world that supports and loves us as opposed to one in which we are on our own.

The following numbers and organizations are but a few that you can reach out to if you don't feel you have someone you can talk to one on one:

National Suicide Prevention Lifeline
1.800.273.8255 (TALK)
National HelpLine
1.800.662.4357 (HELP)
SAMSHA
National Institute of Mental Health
The Trevor Project
Suicide Prevention Resource Center
To Write Love On Her Arms

•

Thank you to my fellow Gentleman Bosses: Derrick C. Brown and Cristin O'Keefe Aptowicz, love you two always. Thank you to Brandon Hinman and AIRSerenbe for the time and space given to me in the fall of 2017, where many of the poems here were able to come out and where this book first took shape. Thank you to Hanif Abdurraqib and Kaveh Akbar for the extra eyes and ears, love that there are wolves joining three of our books. Thank you Naomi Shihab Nye, for you. Thank you to my family for allowing me to learn better over these last four years what family truly means. My love to Linda, Lee, and Jennifer, my heart often thinks of you. Jeff, I miss you every day. 12 years and still it's hard at times to even spell out your name. Forever grateful to have had my life touched by you. Love you always. I hope peace found you. I hope to see you again sometime, someplace.

///

Anis Mojgani is the author of four other books. A two-time National Poetry Slam Champion and winner of the International World Cup Poetry Slam, his work has appeared on HBO, NPR, and in such journals as *Bat City Review*, *Rattle*, *Thrush*, *Muzzle*, and *Forklift Ohio*. Originally from New Orleans, Anis currently lives in Portland, OR.

IF YOU LIKE ANIS MOJGANI, ANIS LIKES...

AMULET
JASON BAYANI

I LOVE SCIENCE
SHANNY JEAN MANEY

THIS WAY TO THE SUGAR
HIEU MINH NGUYEN

THE YEAR OF NO MISTAKES
CRISTIN O'KEEFE APTOWICZ

SLOW DANCE WITH SASQUATCH
JEREMY RADIN

Write Bloody Publishing distributes and promotes great books of poetry every year. We are an independent press dedicated to quality literature and book design.

Our employees are authors and artists so we call ourselves a family. Our design team comes from all over America: modern painters, photographers and rock album designers create book covers we're proud to be judged by.

We are grassroots, D.I.Y., bootstrap believers. Pull up a good book and join the family. Support independent authors, artists and presses.

Want to know more about Write Bloody books, authors and events?
Join our maling list at

www.writebloody.com

WRITE BLOODY BOOKS

After the Witch Hunt — Megan Falley

Aim for the Head: An Anthology of Zombie Poetry — Rob Sturma, Editor

Amulet — Jason Bayani

Any Psalm You Want — Khary Jackson

Birthday Girl with Possum — Brendan Constantine

The Bones Below — Sierra DeMulder

Born in the Year of the Butterfly Knife — Derrick C. Brown

Bouquet of Red Flags — Taylor Mali

Bring Down the Chandeliers — Tara Hardy

Ceremony for the Choking Ghost — Karen Finneyfrock

Clear Out the Static in Your Attic — Rebecca Bridge & Isla McKetta

Counting Descent — Clint Smith

Courage: Daring Poems for Gutsy Girls — Karen Finneyfrock, Mindy Nettifee,
& Rachel McKibbens, Editors

Dear Future Boyfriend — Cristin O'Keefe Aptowicz

Do Not Bring Him Water — Caitlin Scarano

Drunks and Other Poems of Recovery — Jack McCarthy

The Elephant Engine High Dive Revival Anthology

Everyone I Love is a Stranger to Someone Else — Annelyse Gelman

Everything Is Everything — Cristin O'Keefe Aptowicz

Favorite Daughter — Nancy Huang

The Feather Room — Anis Mojgani

Floating, Brilliant, Gone — Franny Choi

Glitter in the Blood: A Guide to Braver Writing — Mindy Nettifee

Good Grief — Stevie Edwards

The Good Things About America — Derrick C. Brown & Kevin Staniec, Editors

The Heart of a Comet — Pages D. Matam

Hello. It Doesn't Matter — Derrick C. Brown

Hot Teen Slut — Cristin O'Keefe Aptowicz

How to Love the Empty Air — Cristin O'Keefe Aptowicz

I Love Science! — Shanny Jean Maney

I Love You Is Back — Derrick C. Brown

The Importance of Being Ernest — Ernest Cline

In Search of Midnight — Mike McGee

WRITEBLOODY
QUALITY AMERICAN BOOKS

Lightning Source UK Ltd.
Milton Keynes UK
UKHW01f155020518
321990UK00001B/367/P